Cats

Carol Kyle

The breed standards that appear in this book are printed directly from the *CFA Show Standards* booklet and appear here through the courtesy of the Cat Fanciers' Association, Inc.

Distributed in the UNITED STATES by T.F.H. Publications, Inc., 211 West Sylvania Avenue, Neptune City, NJ 07753; in CANADA by H & L Pet Supplies Inc., 27 Kingston Crescent, Kitchener, Ontario N2B 2T6; Rolf C. Hagen Ltd., 3225 Sartelon Street, Montreal 382 Quebec; in ENGLAND by T.F.H. Publications Limited, 4 Kier Park, Ascot, Berkshire SL5 7DS; in AUSTRALIA AND THE SOUTH PACIFIC by T.F.H. (Australia) Pty. Ltd., Box 149, Brookvale 2100 N.S.W., Australia; in NEW ZEALAND by Ross Haines & Son, Ltd., 18 Monmouth Street, Grey Lynn, Auckland 2 New Zealand; in SINGAPORE AND MALAYSIA by MPH Distributors (S) Pte., Ltd., 601 Sims Drive, # 03/07/21, Singapore 1438; in the PHILIPPINES by Bio-Research, 5 Lippay Street, San Lorenzo Village, Makati Rizal; in SOUTH AFRICA by Multipet Pty. Ltd., 30 Turners Avenue, Durban 4001. Published by T.F.H. Publications Inc., Ltd. the British Crown Colony of Hong Kong.

Contents

Color photography
Lewis Fineman—poster B.
Jill Wiliams 59.

Poster Captions
Poster A—Havana Brown.
Poster B—Abyssinian.
Poster C—shorthaired tabby.
Poster D—cream Persian.
Poster E—red tabby shorthaired kitten.
Poster F—pair of tabby longhairs.

Black and white illustrations
Lynn Hamilton 26, 29, 31, 34, 39, 41, 47.
E. Hoy title page, 4, 71, 73, 74, 76, 77.
Frank Jackson 5.
Yonnet 79.

American Shorthair tabby. Some of the first domestic cats that appeared thousands of years ago probably exhibited one of the tabby patterns.

History of the Domestic Cat

Of all the animals known to man, wild or domestic, none has been regarded with as much fascination as the cat. History tells us that cats have been both admired and feared; some civilizations worshipped them, while others persecuted them almost to the point of extinction. But one thing is certain: no matter how man has viewed these mysterious creatures—whether as friend or foe—for thousands of years they have shared his world. Actually, cats have been around for millions of years, long before the dawn of recorded history. Those that we see today descended from a small, short-legged, slender-bodied carnivore known as *Miacis*, with whom such mammals as dogs, bears, raccoons, and weasels share a common ancestry. But when was it that cats were first domesticated? That is to say, when did cats begin to live in close association with man, working for him and providing companionship? No one knows for sure; only theories and legends provide us with clues.

Some experts speculate that our earliest records of the cat as a domestic animal, rather than as a wild beast, come from the Egyptians. Through such art forms as tomb painting and sculpture, it is clear that cats were treated with

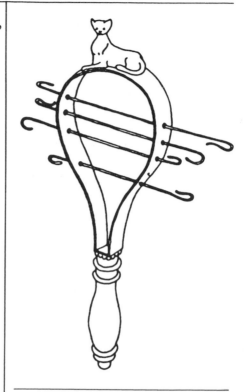

An Egyptian sistrum (a percussion instrument) that was carried by the cat goddess Bastet.

great respect, as were other animals. The fact that cats were mummified also demonstrates that these felines were held in high esteem. They were especially valued for their ability to keep the rodent population down, particularly where food was stored, and they often accompanied their masters on hunting

History of the Domestic Cat

expeditions. The Egyptian goddess Bastet, who was portrayed as part woman and part cat, became an important deity; and it was believed that she bestowed her powers on the cats of Egypt. Thus endowed, these cats were considered sacred and therefore it was prestigious to own one.

The seafaring Phoenicians, despite Egyptian laws forbidding the export of cats, smuggled them aboard ships and traded them along the Mediterranean. And it is likely that wherever Roman armies marched, cats were to be found among their plundered treasures from faraway lands. Still, traders from the Far East, particularly from China and India, often had cats for sale, and for centuries these exotic creatures spread throughout Europe. By the seventeenth century, cats began to appear in America. So the cat made its way to almost every corner of the earth, earning its keep on the farm as exterminator of rodents and other vermin and winning its way into the hearts of aristocrat and peasant alike.

Throughout history, not all accounts of the domestic cat, *Felis catus,* were favorable—not everyone applauded the cat's virtues as companion and hunter. There were myths and superstitions of cats that were evil and brought bad luck to their owners. As early as the thirteenth century, those people suspected of practicing witchcraft were swiftly convicted and sentenced to death along with their cats, often referred to as "familiars" of witches. Thousands of these poor creatures, whose glaring yellow eyes and arched backs covered with bristled fur gave them the appearance of being possessed by the devil, were needlessly tortured and burned.

That was a long time ago. Today we are better educated and not so quick to believe old wives' tales about the good or bad luck a cat brings us; however, to this day there are still mixed feelings about cats. For as many people who love felines, there are lots more who do not trust them, who feel uneasy in their presence. If only these skeptics would try to understand and appreciate the feline mystique and to establish a good rapport with a pet cat, then they would see why through the ages cats have endeared themselves to man as household pet, as friend, as mouser, and as family celebrity.

Understanding the Cat

Cats have been described with all sorts of adjectives, many of which are complimentary. They are beautiful, intelligent, graceful, quiet, and clean; unfortunately, they have been much maligned by those who do not understand feline behavior. Words such as sneaky, unfriendly, independent, and mischievous, when used to describe our furry friends, have created a negative picture. Once you discover that a tiger growls inside every pet kitty that purrs, and that these furry creatures exhibit a large repertoire of complex behaviors—which are largely innate—then a more positive attitude toward felines can develop.

In the wild, cats are skillful hunters with some of the most finely honed senses in all the animal kingdom. Except for lions, which live together in groups, or prides, most species of the family Felidae are solitary by nature, coming together with others of their kind during the breeding season to mate and rear their young. So it might come as no surprise that even domestic cats display behavior similar to that of their wild cousins. Domestic cats can be observed crouching low to the ground with ears perked and eyes fixed on their prey (whether it be a bird, a mouse, or a toy), ready to spring into action more quickly than the wink of an eye. And, like their wild relatives, many pet cats prefer to be left alone, deciding for themselves what times are appropriate for play and social activities. Kittens often act out predatory instincts through play, as they stalk a littermate, bat with their paws, pounce, run, and jump.

The cat is a complicated creature, always a few steps ahead of us. We can never be sure we are master, as we are with dogs, for example. But in spite of the cat's aloofness and apparent self-sufficiency, our love and attention can make of these pets warm and lasting friends. In every cat is a curious, lively kitten. The cat is full of fun, but never undignified; it is often a clown, but never a fool. Learn to appreciate its keen abilities, understand its weaknesses and peculiar temperament, and it won't be long before you find the two of you living together in perfect harmony for many years.

What Kind of Cat?

There is a cat to suit almost everyone's preferences, but before you decide to own one, there are a number of questions that need answering before you make a final decision. Do you want a purebred, pedigreed cat that has been raised by a breeder and developed according to a standard of perfection for its particular breed? Or would you settle for a mixed breed of cat from your neighbor's recent litter? Perhaps you should visit a local animal shelter that takes in stray cats, nurses them back to health, inoculates them, alters them so that they cannot breed indiscriminately and fill the world with unwanted kittens, and, of course, finds suitable homes for them. There are longhaired and shorthaired cats, dozens of breeds to choose from, and an infinite number of color varieties and coat patterns to consider. Some people want a male; others prefer a female. Should you start with a kitten or an adult? If you select a longhaired cat, such as a Persian, a Maine Coon, or a Somali, will you have the time to groom its long fur each day? Do you plan to show your cat in competition with other cats? All of these questions are important in helping you locate the pet cat of your dreams.

In some cat registering associations, the predominance of white in this black and white bi-color American Shorthair would be considered a show fault; therefore, most breeders would classify this cat as pet-quality.

Most reputable breeders can sell you a purebred, pet-quality animal with all of its credentials, *i.e.*, pedigree, registration papers, health records, inoculation certificates, and so on, *if* you agree to have the cat neutered (if it is a male) or spayed (if it is a female). In this way, they can protect themselves and their cattery reputations from buyers who might knowingly or unknowingly allow these pet-quality animals to breed and thereby perpetuate inferior animals with undesirable qualities, according to the breed standard. Most breeders care about their cats and want to see them placed in loving homes with responsible owners. They also want

What Kind of Cat?

to be certain that their show-quality cats are sold to owners who will allow these animals to reach their highest potential in the show ring. Similarly, breeders want to know that their breeder-quality queens and studs (unaltered female and male breeder cats) will be used in reputable breeding programs to improve their particular breed. Breeder cats may produce many show-quality offspring, although they themselves may not be winners at the shows. Purebred cats, whether pet- breeder- or show-quality, may be expensive, but generally you can be assured of a healthy animal whose qualities and ancestry can be guaranteed.

The Siamese breed is quite popular among cat fanciers; besides the original seal point variety, other point colors can be seen today.

The Purebred Cat

Most breeders of purebred cats classify their animals in one of three categories: pet, breeder, or show. Their pet-quality stock is usually composed of kittens and cats that are in no way any less healthy or attractive than their breeder- or show-quality specimens; the reason these animals are placed as pets is because when evaluated against a particular cat registering association's rigid breed standard, they just don't measure up. For example, some associations would disqualify an Abyssinian that has gray undercoat anywhere on its body. In Russian Blues, any evidence of tabby markings is usually a fault in the show ring as is a mask that extends over the head in Himalayans. But these so-called flaws are often so subtle that they go unnoticed to the untrained eye. There is no such thing as a perfect cat; breeders can only strive for perfection, using the breed standard as an ideal. So these kittens and cats that neither have the potential to compete at shows nor have the desirable traits that a good producer or breeder cat would are instead sold as pets.

What Kind of Cat?

The Mixed Breed

There are plenty of feline candidates to choose from that are not purebred and pedigreed. Mixed breeds are cats that have been randomly bred; that is to say, several breeds may have been intermixed (mongrelized). An example of this is a cat that looks as though it might be part Persian—it has rather longish fur and short, stocky legs—but it may not exhibit all of the other typical features that a purebred Persian would, such as the round, massive head, or the small ears set wide apart and low on the head, or the short, snub nose. No genetic principles were studied, no pedigrees were scrutinized, no breeding strategies were carefully formulated to produce the mixed breed; in fact, of all the cats that live in your city or town, most of them probably fall into the mixed breed category. These cats, incidentally, can be shown at cat shows in the special household pet division, apart from purebred, pedigreed animals. They are judged solely on their beauty and condition, with no regard to a breed standard of perfection. Pedigreed, on the other hand, refers to an animal that has at least three generations of pure breeding behind it (its ancestors are not mongrels or mixed breeds), and this information is usually recorded with an official cat registering association.

Male or Female?

Both sexes of cats have the potential to be good companions; however, before deciding on a male or female cat, behavior should be considered. Keep in mind that each cat will develop its own personality and that one can only generalize about differences between male and female behavior. As they reach sexual maturity, males that have not been neutered tend to wander, to get into fights with other tom cats (especially over females in heat), and to spray urine on various objects to mark their territory. This is perfectly normal behavior for an unneutered, sexually mature tom; nonetheless, this normal behavior can try the nerves of even the most patient person and dedicated cat lover. The urine of a male can be particularly offensive; it can permeate every corner in your home. But many a cat owner learns to live with a spraying tom. Others opt for neutering their males, since in most cases this procedure reduces and even eliminates their tendency

What Kind of Cat?

toward aggression and spraying. All cats, whether male or female, should be altered if they are not intended to be used for breeding. In this way, they will not contribute to an already overpopulated world of felines. Altered cats also make better pets, since they are not preoccupied with members of the opposite sex.

Sexually mature female cats tend to be less aggressive toward other cats than males. Yes, a mother cat guided by maternal instincts will fight tooth and nail for her kittens, especially if she feels that their security has been threatened in any way. But generally females do not look for fights the way males do. Females, whether spayed or unspayed, are less likely to spray urine, although this does sometimes occur. Then, of course, there is the mating season. A female cat in heat can be difficult to live with, as she cries and demands to be let out to meet with any and all available toms. She becomes restless and difficult to handle. And then there is the matter of pregnancy and of being able to find homes for her kittens. All of this should be considered before bringing an unspayed, sexually mature female cat into your home.

Adult or Kitten?

There is nothing wrong with wanting to secure an adult cat as a companion; however, since cats tend to be creatures of habit and since sometimes you can't teach an old cat new tricks, you would probably do well with a kitten about eight to ten weeks old. By eight weeks, provided a kitten has been raised by its mother in the company of its littermates and not deprived of maternal nurturing, a kitten should be self-feeding, properly socialized, and ready to be weaned from its mother. And, if mother cat herself was litter pan trained, chances are that by eight weeks her kittens will have learned this behavior also. Before selecting a kitten, it would be wise to ask the seller if it has been trained to use a litter pan. A kitten may seem timid when you bring it home in its little box or carrier, but with love and patience, soon it will come to regard your home as its own. Also, kittens can be trained to learn what is acceptable behavior and what is not in their new home. A kitten is fun; it's exciting to watch it grow.

Of course, if you are interested in purchasing a purebred show-quality kitten, then you will probably have to wait until the kitten is older than eight to ten weeks. It is not uncommon for breeders to wait until they can accurately determine a cat's show potential, and often a show kitten is not released until a breeder is certain of this. The age at which a purebred kitten is released to its new owner depends on the breed of cat and its individual development.

Whether you want to start your own breeding program or breed your household pet, you will want an adult cat, not a kitten, that is sexually mature and unaltered. A veterinarian can determine whether your male or female cat has reached the proper breeding age. Cat breeding, however, is not for beginners.

Longhaired or Shorthaired?

Cats are often grouped according to hair length; simply, they are either longhaired or shorthaired. The prospective cat owner should consider this, particularly with the former group. While all cats need some grooming attention from their owners, even though they keep themselves pretty clean, the longhaired breeds need special care. Unless their fur is brushed each day, unsightly tangled and matted hair will result. There is also the consideration of shedding. In the spring and fall, most cats shed their hair; with some breeds, the fur goes unnoticed, but with others— especially the longhaired ones—there may be remnants of fur all over the house. Also, the hair of a longhaired cat may get soiled more often than that of a shorthaired cat, so careful attention will have to be paid to this. For some longhaired breeds, this means regular bath sessions.

Indoor or Outdoor Cat?

Many people do not realize that a cat or kitten is perfectly happy to live as an indoor cat, provided that it has room to walk, run, and exercise. It should not be confined to a cage; however, it need not have free access to the entire house. Perhaps it could be kept in the family room or confined to a particular section of the house. In any case, the animal should not be isolated from the rest of the family. Go into its living area often and visit with it, play with it, talk to it, make it feel like part of the family. Cats are independent, but they do not want to be left alone all of the time; they need attention from you. By all means, do not keep the

What Kind of Cat?

animal in your garage where there are all sorts of chemicals, sharp tools, and exhaust fumes that could be harmful to your pet. And don't isolate it in a dark, dank cellar either. The cat or kitten needs fresh air and sunshine, which it need not get outdoors. A sunny room that is well ventilated will do.

The question of whether to let a cat or kitten outdoors is a controversial one. They do enjoy lying in the sun on the backyard deck or walking through the grass. But if your property is not enclosed by means of a fence or a wall, or the like, there is a possibility that your pet will take to wandering. Oh, it probably will find its way home again, but then again it may not. It might get lost, or it might be hit by a car, or mauled by an unleashed dog, or poisoned by some sadistic person, or stolen. At the very least, it might injure itself or get its coat dirty. All of these considerations are valid reasons for keeping your dearly beloved cat or kitten inside the house where it will be safe from harm, where it will be supervised by you most of the time. (You will find that most show cats are indoor cats for the same reasons mentioned.) Besides considering the harm that might befall your pet, think about all of those unwanted kittens that

result from unaltered cats that are allowed to roam the neighborhood. An outdoor cat especially should be altered if it is not intended for breeding.

If you do insist on keeping your pet outdoors, make certain that it cannot roam beyond the boundaries of your yard or property. Keep the animal in a large pen or run, or fence in the yard. Take these precautionary measures if you really love your cat. In many cities and towns there are laws prohibiting dog *and* cat owners from allowing their pets to run loose in the neighborhood unleashed and unsupervised. Many people are unaware of the law as it applies to cats because rarely is it enforced; but keep in mind that in some municipalities, you may be fined if an animal control officer finds your roaming feline or if a neighbor complains about your negligence as a pet owner.

Selecting a Cat

Where to Look

Catteries are a great place to find healthy, well-cared-for felines. The breeders who own or manage these establishments usually are quite knowledgeable about the stock that they have for sale, and breeders of purebred cats can offer pet-breeder- or show-quality cats, depending on what you want. Prices will vary depending on the quality of the animal, its genetic background, its family history of champions and grand champions, its show potential, and so on. Or visit a cat show; there you will find a great number of breeders at one time, and you will be able to see firsthand some of the finest representatives of purebred cats around.

There are national, state, and local organizations dedicated to animal welfare, *i.e.,* animal shelters, pet adoption agencies, and humane societies. Staffed by people who really love cats and who want to see them placed in happy homes, these are sources worth considering. Veterinarians usually have useful information regarding the procurement of a cat or kitten. They might be able to put you in touch with a client of theirs, with a breeder, or with a local cat club or cat registering organization. Pet shops are another possibility. Visit several and evaluate how clean the premises is and how healthy and active the animals are. Talk to the owner or store personnel to find out just how informed and concerned they are about their feline residents. If a pet shop does not have the particular cat or kitten that you want, perhaps they can get one for you. Cats and kittens are also advertised in the Classified sections of newspapers, in magazines that are devoted to cats, and on shopping mall bulletin boards. Before you decide where to look for a cat or kitten, look around and evaluate all of the options.

Signs of Good Health

No matter what source you visit to find a cat or kitten, whether it be a cattery, an animal shelter, a pet shop, or a neighbor, be absolutely certain that you select a *healthy* animal. Good health cannot be overemphasized here. Below are criteria on which you should base your decision to select a cat or kitten. As mentioned earlier, if you want a kitten, question the seller about its age. Kittens younger than eight weeks generally should not be separated from their mother and

Selecting a Cat

To accurately sex a kitten, you must lift its tail. In males, the distance between the anal and penile openings will be greater, whereas in females, the distance between the anal and vulval openings is not so great.

littermates. If you want a cat for breeding, make sure it is sexually mature and that it has not been altered. The seller should be able to tell you if the cat is old enough to be bred.

Give the cat or kitten you are interested in a quick physical examination to determine its condition. Ask the seller to hold this animal so that you can examine it closely. Its eyes should be clear and bright, free of tears, dirt, or foreign matter. Its nose should be clean, not runny. The condition of the coat is an important indicator of the

animal's general health, since it keeps itself impeccably groomed by using its tongue to lick and clean the fur. Whether longhaired or shorthaired, the coat should be soft, smooth, and shiny. A dirty, matted coat and a ragged appearance indicates that the cat or kitten probably is not feeling well and is therefore neglecting to groom itself. The ears should be clean; if there is dirt or dark matter inside the ears, suspect the presence of ear mites and avoid this animal. Why start with problems? Ask the seller to open the cat's or kitten's mouth. Check the teeth to see that all are there, intact, and unbroken. The gums should be pink, smooth, and free of sores. Check beneath the tail; the anus should be clean and free of fecal matter. If this area is dirty (that is to say, if the fur in this area is soiled, matted, and wet) make another selection. This cat or kitten probably has diarrhea, which is a symptom of any one of a variety of problems. Check the underlying skin in random places to see that it is free of fleas, ticks, or mites. At the same time check to see that there are no sores or lumps.

Make sure that your examination includes an observation of how the animal moves. It should walk and run without difficulty. Its breathing

Selecting a Cat

should be slow and rhythmic, not labored. And try to observe the cat's or kitten's behavior as much as possible. If you are interested in a kitten, chances are that you will be able to watch how it interacts with its littermates. Normal kittens are active and playful and curious about their environment. You might want to pull a string along the floor to see how the kitten responds. No normal kitten can resist a bit of string. You might also want to approach the kitten from behind and clap your hands to test its hearing. Whether a cat or a kitten, its overall appearance should be one of an active and alert animal.

Notice the environment in which the cat or kitten was raised. You can get a pretty good impression of how clean and healthy the animal is by looking at its surroundings. And be sure to ask lots of questions. A seller who really cares about his or her cats and their placement in good homes should welcome all inquiries that you might have. If a cat or kitten seems abnormal in any way, select another animal. It is easy to fall in love with the runt of the litter or to feel sorry for a cat that is plagued with fleas, but these animals probably will cause problems later and cost you more than you bargained for.

When you have made your decision and have selected a particular cat or kitten, find out from the seller what food it is accustomed to, what inoculations it has had, and ask to see any health records that are available. If you are buying a purebred, pedigreed animal, you should expect to secure its registration papers, in addition to health certificates, upon purchase. Of course, as already mentioned, most breeders of purebred, pet-quality cats and kittens will render these documents only after the pet has been altered. Make sure all agreements are made prior to the purchase.

Color Captions
Domestic shorthaired tabby, page 17. Russian Blue; brilliant green eyes are characteristic of this breed, page 18. A red tabby shorthair enjoys its meal beneath a shady tree, page 19. Purebred kittens, in this case seal point Siamese, are bred according to a rigid standard of perfection, pages 20 and 21. Kittens love to explore everything in the home, even gift wrappings, page 22. This is not a white Persian kitten; the black eye rims indicate that it is a chinchilla, page 23. This pair of longhaired kittens strikes a familiar pose in front of a goldfish bowl!, page 24.

Bringing the Cat Home

Cat-Proofing Your Home

Just prior to bringing your new cat or kitten home, scan every room in the house and remove or put into storage those things that you feel might be dangerous to keep around your pet. Some things are more obvious than others, but here are a few suggestions of what to look for. Certain houseplants can be deadly if your cat or kitten should happen to nibble on and swallow them. Check with a veterinarian or with a local garden center to find out which plants are safe and which are not to keep around cats. Philodendron, dieffenbachia, mistletoe, poppies, and ivy are but a few of the ones that are poisonous to cats. There are all sorts of poisons around the house in the form of household detergents, cleaning fluids, solvents, and the like. Be sure to keep these items far from your pet's reach. The kitchen alone can be a danger zone for a cat. It might climb, unnoticed, into an open refrigerator or dishwasher and be shut in. Or it might jump on top of a hot stove or cut itself on a sharp utensil sitting on a counter top. Or it might walk across a kitchen floor freshly mopped with chemical detergent and then lick its feet clean. Cats have been known to

PRIVET
(*Ligustrum vulgare*)

Many plants, both inside and outside of the home, are poisonous to cats; these include the privet, the yew, and the monkshood.

MONKSHOOD, ACONITE
(*Aconitum* spp.)

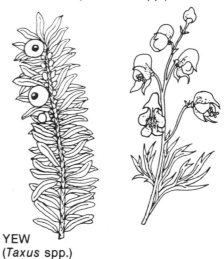

YEW
(*Taxus* spp.)

Bringing the Cat Home

chew on electrical wires and swallow small objects, such as bits of string or plastic. The list could go on. They can get into quite a bit of mischief, especially when you are not there to supervise them. If you really care about that cat or kitten who is about to take up residence with you, then make every effort to check these potential dangers *before* it arrives in its new home. Think of this creature as you would a small child, and prepare for its arrival accordingly.

Acclimation

Bear in mind that whether you bring a timid kitten or a self-confident cat into your home, the animal will have to gradually adjust to its new environment. Everyone will want to hold the new family member, pet it, talk to it, play with it, and give it a tour of the house. But it is wiser, especially from the animal's point of view, to let it explore by itself. Place the new resident alone in a quiet room and keep the door slightly open. A small dish of its favorite food (the seller should know this), a water dish, and a litter pan should be set up in the room. Let the animal eat in peace and quiet, if it is in the mood to do so, and allow it to decide when a good time is to come out to investigate the rest of the house. Before you know it, the cat will be rubbing against your legs, purring with contentment, ready to move in with bag and baggage.

With a kitten especially, remember to be gentle. Don't chase after it; instead, let it come to you. After all, for this little creature, going to a new home is quite an adventure. Everything, yourself included, will seem overwhelmingly large. It seeks the security it once knew with its mother and siblings. Avoid making loud noises or sudden movements that might frighten the kitten. These first few days are vitally important and may determine whether the two of you will be able

A kitten may seem shy at first in its new home; with love and patience, you can make it feel like part of the family.

Bringing the Cat Home

to live together under the same roof.

Once your new cat or kitten is relaxed, eating, and washing itself, try holding it on your lap, although never against its will. Gently stroke the animal; but if it wants to jump down, let it do so. Don't give the cat the impression that your lap is some kind of trap. The warmth of your body and the sound of your voice should give the cat a sense of security. Gradually you will be able to play with your new companion, but don't overdo it yet. Kittens, particularly, tire easily.

Litter Pan Training

Most cats are already litter pan trained, but this is not always the case with a kitten. Since it requires time and effort on your part to teach the kitten this important aspect of feline personal hygiene, it makes sense to bring home only a kitten that has been trained, either by its mother or by its former owner, to use the litter pan. Litter pan training should begin immediately after the kitten has settled into its new home and eaten its first meal. After each meal, after each rest period, and after each vigorous play session, place the kitten in the litter pan. Hold its

front paws and make scratching motions. Be patient; give the kitten time to do its business, and by all means do not use force. In due time the kitten will learn the desired behavior. But don't be surprised if you find yourself cleaning up after it a number of times until it masters the litter pan technique.

Litter pans are available in a variety of shapes and sizes, and any one of the commercially-made cat litters can then be used to fill whichever pan you choose. Select a litter pan that is sturdy and won't tip over, one that is made of washable material, and one that is large enough to accommodate a mature cat. Select a suitable place for the litter pan (not too close to the animal's food and water dishes) and keep it there at all times so that your cat or kitten goes to the same place each time it has to relieve itself. In a large house, it might be a good idea to strategically position two or more litter pans, perhaps one on each level, in a house with many stories.

Obviously it is up to you to keep the litter pan clean. Cats are very fussy about their toilet habits and their litter pans. They have been known not to use a dirty pan, preferring instead to soil the carpet or the floor. The solid waste should

Bringing the Cat Home

be removed daily from the litter pan (a litter strainer or a large strainer-spoon set aside just for this purpose is handy), and it should be flushed down the toilet or disposed of in some other appropriate way. The moistened litter material should be stirred up from the bottom of the pan and more litter (new material) should be added and mixed in. The litter should be changed often, and the pan itself should be washed and sterilized regularly.

There are various ways to control litter pan odors: baking soda sprinkled on the bottom of the pan can help; special odor-absorbing litters are commercially available, as are special preparations that can be added to litter; and of course there are even covered litter pans with built-in filtering systems. Whichever method you use to help control and eliminate litter pan odors, remember that your cat or kitten may not accept the idea at first. You may have to experiment with different litters and products before the animal agrees to use its litter-filled pan. And keep in mind that some litters designed to control odors, particularly colored ones, may stain your cat or kitten's coat. This could be disastrous for a show animal. Avoid using such non-commercial litters as sand, soil, sawdust, and

newspaper. While these materials may cost you nothing or next to nothing, they are not recommended. Sand or soil may contain microorganisms that spread disease or that may be annoying to your pet, while sawdust and newspaper do not have the absorbent properties that commercial litters do.

If your living conditions are such that your cat or kitten can come and go as it pleases in and out-of-doors, so much the better. Litter pan training is unnecessary in this instance. Simply show the cat or kitten the spot outdoors that you prefer it to use as its toilet, and dig its front paws into the earth a few times. Some cat owners even cut a small porthole in their back door, hinging it so that it swings both ways; this makes it easier for their cats to come and go. Keep in mind that if your pet is let outside, it should be confined to a pen or a fenced-in yard; otherwise, it may tend to roam away from the house, where all sorts of dangers await it.

Home Sweet Home

Once your kitten is acclimated and using its litter pan, or using the outdoors as its toilet facility, select a spot in your home that the animal

Bringing the Cat Home

can call its own. Later, the cat or kitten will undoubtedly discover a few more places where it can be alone; however, in the beginning it is important that there be one permanent place where its bed can be placed. (There are a great number of beds and baskets available; if you shop around, you are sure to find just the right one for your cat or kitten.) This location should be free from drafts, extreme temperatures, and household commotion. This special place might be near a sunny window ledge, in a cozy corner, or in an old, comfortable chair. Wherever it is, encourage your pet to spend time there.

Cats love the great outdoors, where they can climb and explore their surroundings; however, it is best to keep your cat indoors, away from dangers that may await it outside.

Cats and Children

It is fine for children to have cats and kittens as pets; however, before your feline pet sets foot (or rather paw) in its new home, there are a few things you, as a responsible cat owner, should make clear to the younger members of the family. First of all, the cat or kitten is not a plaything; it is a living creature that needs to be cared for. It will become a member of the family and will have to share the family's living space. It is important to explain to children that they should not tease or torment the animal: pet it, yes; play its favorite games, yes.

Teach children the proper way to pick up and hold a cat or kitten. Show them how to approach the animal gently and quietly. Bend down, grasp the animal under its front paws with your forearm, fingers extending toward the cat's or kitten's neck. As you begin to lift the animal, quickly support its rear end by holding the back paws with your other hand and by pressing the animal against your body. Be certain to hold the cat or kitten firmly so that it has proper support. It is

29

Bringing the Cat Home

important for children to learn the correct procedure so that they do not hurt the animal and so that they do not hurt themselves in the process. Emphasize that the cat or kitten should *never* be lifted by its tail and it should *never* be lifted under its front paws without support under its backside. Practice with the child so he or she understands how to pick up and hold the cat. Actually, the child should avoid picking up the animal too often; sometimes the cat prefers to be alone, and it may dislike too much handling.

When the new cat or kitten arrives in your home, explain to the children that the pet must be left alone for awhile until it becomes accustomed to its new surroundings. When it feels at home, it will become more sociable as it discovers all of the family members. Give it time to adjust. If you let the children handle the cat or kitten too much upon arrival, it will only become more frightened; in fact, it may take longer for the animal to make the adjustment to its new home. As the new pet becomes acclimated, perhaps the children can share in the responsibilities of keeping it fed and groomed. This is a great way for children to learn how to care for another living thing.

One way to restrain your cat or kitten when it is outdoors is with a collar and leash. These items are handy in the event you want to take the cat or kitten for a walk.

Sometimes all it takes is a rattle of the food can to get your cats or kittens to come home in time for dinner. ➡

General Care of the Cat

When you take a cat into your home, you take on certain responsibilities. But since the cat is such a self-sufficient creature, these responsibilities are easy to fulfill. Your basic obligations are to supply your cat with a well-balanced diet and fresh water, to provide a comfortable place for it to sleep, to groom it regularly, to protect it from harm, and to see to it that it remains healthy. Be kind, be loving, but do not spoil the cat. Both of you will suffer from spoiling, and you will have no one to blame but yourself.

Feeding

A proper diet is essential in order to keep your cat or kitten healthy. The animal's dietary needs will change throughout its lifetime, as it grows from a kitten to an adult and from an adult to an older cat. Cats in breeding condition, lactating females, and sick cats have special needs, about which the veterinarian can guide you.

As already mentioned, ask the seller about the cat's or kitten's diet,

31

General Care of the Cat

and try to duplicate it for a few days until it feels at home. If you plan to switch foods, gradually mix in the new food each day until the transition is complete. You will find that the new member of the family seems to have a huge appetite but a small capacity for food. At feeding time, give the animal as much as it will eat and remove any leftovers (particularly canned cat food).

Kittens grow at a rapid rate and expend a great deal of energy during the course of a day, so it is important to feed them small portions several times a day. As they mature, fewer portions will suffice. A well-balanced diet of protein, carbohydrates, fat, vitamins, minerals, and water will ensure proper growth. Avoid offering a one-sided diet; that is, one that consists primarily of fish or beef liver. Too much of any one food may actually be harmful. And be sure to offer only fresh food. Milk is a controversial food: too much may cause diarrhea in some cats and kittens that are sensitive to it. When in doubt, check with a veterinarian.

There are plenty of nutritionally complete and balanced commercial food preparations available for cats. Be sure to read all labels before you make your purchase. There are canned cat foods, which seem to be especially palatable, but which cost more than some other types of cat foods. These canned foods also spoil easily, so they cannot be left in the feeding dish for long periods of time. Then there are the semi-moist foods, most of which come in moisture-proof packages. These tend to be slightly less expensive than the canned foods, have less moisture content, and can be left out in the cat's feeding dish for longer intervals. Finally there are dry foods. These usually are hard morsels that can be left out all day, overnight, and even over a weekend. Every few days, however, this food should be replaced with a fresh supply. Often, cat owners offer these dry foods as a snack or treat for good behavior. This last group of commercial cat foods is probably the least expensive. To rely on any one kind of food (canned, semi-moist, or dry) may not be desirable; perhaps it is wise to offer all three at different times. The dry foods are certainly convenient, but because they lack moisture, the cat may need to drink more water than usual; an advantage of dry food is that it helps to keep the cat's teeth clean, whereas canned food often sticks to the teeth.

Water should be available at all times, and it should be clean, fresh,

General Care of the Cat

and cool.

Feeding dishes and water dishes should be kept scrupulously clean. Each day they should be washed with soap and hot water, rinsed, and dried. (In fact, when canned food is given, the feeding dish should be washed after every meal.) Surplus canned and semi-moist foods that have been opened should be stored in the refrigerator. Cats prefer food at room temperature. Avoid offering food that has just come from the refrigerator; likewise, never offer hot foods, for fear of burning the cat's or kitten's mouth.

Vitamin and mineral supplements are available commercially; most pet shops stock them. You might try adding them to your pet's food; however, if you are feeding the animal a well-balanced diet, usually this is unnecessary. It wouldn't hurt to seek the advice of a veterinarian in this instance.

Pregnant female cats need extra nutrients for the kittens they are carrying inside them. Feed them plenty of food, especially those foods that are high in calcium. Calcium is important for the kittens' bone development and for building a supply of milk in the queen's mammary glands so that she can nurse her young. Before altering a queen's diet, consult a veterinarian.

As cats mature to old age, they become less active, so it is important to control their intake of food. Altered cats especially are inclined to gain weight, so be careful not to overfeed them. A routine physical examination by a veterinarian will determine what the nutritional needs are for your older cat.

Grooming

When they are healthy, cats are fastidious about keeping themselves groomed. In fact, they spend a great deal of time each day engaged in this important activity. They lick their fur until it is soft and lustrous. They wet their paws with the tongue and then proceed to wash their faces. Cats that are depressed and not well fail to keep their coats in good condition and often exhibit a scruffy appearance. But despite the fact that all cats are extremely clean animals, they will need some attention from their owners. It is wise to start grooming the animal as soon as possible; this is especially easy if you have purchased a kitten. After a few sessions, your cat or kitten will grow to enjoy the experience and even look forward to it.

Brushing and combing are an

General Care of the Cat

important part of the grooming routine; both shorthaired and longhaired cats benefit from this. The latter will need to be brushed and combed every day without fail in order to keep the long hair from tangling. If you neglect a few tangles, then they will develop into large matted areas and it will be almost impossible to deal with them. So it makes sense to groom the longhaired cat *every* day, rather than to skip a day and have to spend extra time in the next session smoothing out the fur. Shorthaired cats should be brushed and combed regularly, perhaps every other day. By brushing and combing the cat's coat, you help to remove loose hairs that otherwise might be swallowed by your pet as it licks its fur. If too

This basketful of longhaired kittens awaits its daily grooming session. Their long coats are brushed and combed each day, and they have come to accept this grooming ritual as part of the normal routine.

much hair is ingested, tight wads—known as hairballs—may develop in the stomach or the intestines. These wads of hair may cause problems for the cat. Should your pet have difficulty with hairballs, there are commercial preparations that dissolve these obstructions so that they can be passed through the cat's rectum. A daily brushing and combing will help control the hairball problem.

There are various kinds of brushes, combs, and other grooming aids available in most pet shops. Ask

General Care of the Cat

the pet dealer to recommend those tools that will be suitable for your particular cat. A hard-rubber brush and a fine-toothed comb work well for shorthaired cats. Brush the entire coat vigorously (against the grain) to loosen the dead hair, and then follow through with the comb to remove the loose hairs. Finally, with the hands, smooth down the coat, rubbing hard so that it lies flat. Your cat should enjoy this! With a longhaired cat, careful attention is needed. This will require more time for the cat owner. Always start by combing the long hair with a blunt-end comb with wide-set teeth. Gently work out any knots and tangles, and be sure to comb underneath the chin, down the chest, inside the front and back legs, and around the tail. Then use a medium-toothed comb to remove small knots, to smooth out the fur, and to remove dead hair. Finally, a fine-toothed comb will help remove dirt and fleas (if there are any). This comb is also especially useful for the hair around the cat's face. A gentle brushing with a soft, natural-bristled brush should follow. Of course, a longhaired show cat needs even more attention, as every hair must be in place.

The cat's eyes, ears, feet, and claws should be carefully examined during each grooming session. Occasionally cats get dust or dirt in the corners of their eyes, and, of course, there is mucus that builds up. All can be easily removed with a damp cotton swab. If you notice an inflammation of the eye or scratches, notify a veterinarian as soon as possible. Clean the ears regularly with a cotton swab, but be careful not to probe too deeply into the inner ear. Gently remove any dirt or wax that has accumulated. If the ears are lined with dark, crusty patches, then there is a chance the cat has ear mites. For this problem, seek professional assistance. Check the feet for cuts, and examine the cat's claws to see if they need to be

Periodically you may have to trim your cat's claws. Claw clippers, made especially for cats, are available at most pet shops.

General Care of the Cat

trimmed. With a pair of claw clippers, trim the overgrown tips, being careful not to cut into the pink area that contains blood vessels which nourish the claw. Clipping the claws is not painful for the cat; it is similar to cutting one's own nails.

Most cats do not like to be bathed; however, there are those cat owners who admit that their pets don't mind this particular grooming routine at all. Show cats will need to be bathed regularly; in fact, many need a bath prior to every show so that they are presented in the best possible condition. Their owners accustom them to bathing when they are young so that they will accept this as the normal routine. This is good advice even if you do not own a show cat. Some owners use dry shampoos or talcum powder; this is especially useful for a longhaired cat. The powder, when sprinkled into the hair, absorbs the excess natural oils of the coat, so that dirt and dust won't cling to it. But if a wet bath is inevitable, here are a few pointers to keep in mind. First, place a rubber mat in the bottom of a large sink or tub and then partially fill it with warm water. Next, place the cat inside, holding it steady while reassuring it with loving words. Wet the cat with water and a soft washcloth. Apply a mild shampoo made especially for cats and work up a good lather, being careful not to get shampoo in the animal's eyes. Rinse the cat with warm water (a short hose with a spray nozzle is good), making sure all traces of shampoo are removed from the coat. Lift the cat from the bath water and place it on a table or counter top. With a large, absorbent towel, give the shorthaired cat a brisk rubdown; pat dry the longhaired cat. You can allow the coat to dry naturally (if you keep the cat away from the cold or from drafts), or you can try using a blow dryer (select a low setting). When the cat has completely dried, it will need to be brushed and combed. For many people, bathing a cat is not as easy as it might seem. You might want to get someone to help you. After a little practice, though, it will become easier, And don't forget to praise your cat for its good behavior.

The Scratching Post

Layers of skin surrounding a cat's claws are continually being shed. Scratching facilitates this process; therefore, it is not uncommon to see a cat digging its claws into something to help loosen these

General Care of the Cat

particles. As previously mentioned, it is important to periodically check your cat's claws; if they are overgrown, trim them with claw clippers made for cats. Another way to help keep the claws trim—and at the same time protect your furniture, draperies, and carpeting—is to provide your cat or kitten with a scratching post. These are available commercially (most pet shops carry them), or you can build your own. Either way, you will be happy to have one. There are a variety of scratching post models, but all serve the same purpose: to offer kitty an acceptable place to scratch. Some are carpet-covered structures, while others may consist of a wooden log fastened to a base. The one you select should be sturdy, so that your cat can stretch out against it without worrying about whether it will tip over. If you have brought a kitten home, introduce it to the scratching post soon after it is acclimated. Hold the kitten up to the post; grasp its front paws and make scratching motions on the post. Soon the kitten will learn the desired behavior. It might take longer to train a mature cat to use the scratching post than a kitten, but it can be done. Repeat often the same procedure used with a kitten.

Cat Accessories

Pet shops are good sources for all of the cat care products that you might need. Here you will find such items as cat beds, toys, carriers, collars, leashes, and harnesses, in addition to other things. For each of these items, there are several styles and prices from which to choose. As mentioned earlier, your cat or kitten deserves its own special place in the house that it can call its own; it is there that its bed or sleeping basket can be placed. Select an appropriate location as your cat's sleeping quarters and encourage your pet to retreat to this spot whenever it feels like resting. An extra cushion or towel or small blanket inside the cat's bed might provide extra comfort. Be sure to select a bed that can be easily cleaned and washed.

Your cat or kitten certainly will appreciate a few toys, but these should not be a substitute for your love and attention. Each day, spend a little time with your pet, and soon you will discover what its favorite games are. Play is important for the cat or kitten's health; it is good exercise as well as mentally stimulating. Select only those toys that are safe for cats; in this matter, a pet dealer can be of assistance. Avoid toys with small parts that could be broken or

General Care of the Cat

chewed off and then swallowed by your pet. Also, be careful with any toy with a dangling string attached to it. Although you and your cat may enjoy a game of "tease" with such a toy, your cat should never be left alone to play with it; your cat might eat the string (swallowed string, just like a swallowed toy part could play havoc with your pet's digestive system) or become entangled in it.

A portable cat carrier is useful, especially when you plan to travel to the veterinarian, to a cat show, or to a vacation spot. The carrier should be large enough to accommodate the animal, sturdy, and well ventilated so that your cat or kitten will be comfortable during its trip. An effective way to accustom your cat or kitten to sitting in its carrier is to place it on the floor, opened. The cat surely will want to explore this enticing hideaway, and if this procedure is repeated often enough, the cat will not resent being confined for short intervals during transit. Show cats, especially, should learn at an early age to accept confinement to their carriers, since they will spend a great deal of time there during their show careers.

Collars, leashes, and harnesses are necessary if you need to restrain your cat. If it is not possible to confine your cat or kitten outdoors in a pen or fenced-in backyard, for example, then it should be kept on a leash so that it cannot roam or run away. A leash comes in handy if you want to take your cat for a walk, and it can be fastened to either a collar or a harness. Some collars are designed to hold identification tags (these are useful in case your cat or kitten gets lost), while others help keep fleas away. Some cat owners prefer to use the leash with a harness rather than a collar, since it offers more restraint. Cats have been known to slip out of collars. Try to avoid placing a collar or harness on a show cat; sometimes these accessories damage the coat.

One other item that you might want to purchase for your cat or kitten is catnip. It is a plant that almost all cats love, and when sniffed or chewed, it has an intoxicating effect. A pinch of catnip will be rolled on, tossed, rubbed, and pawed until it is taken away. Catnip can be bought in loose form; sometimes it is sewn into toys. Offer it as a special treat to reward good behavior. Some cat owners attach a catnip-filled toy to a scratching post to entice their pets to scratch this device instead of the furniture.

Keeping the Cat Healthy

Responsibilities of the Owner

When you decide to share your life with a cat or kitten, you must keep it healthy by offering it a proper diet, grooming assistance, medical care, love, attention, and a safe, warm home. When these conditions are met, your pet should thrive and bring you many happy years of cat ownership. Part of your duty as a cat owner is to observe your cat or kitten regularly. Learn to know what is "normal" for your pet. A cat *can* become ill or suffer from a parasite infestation. If you suspect something is seriously wrong, contact a veterinarian as soon as possible. But don't call the vet over every little thing. For example, if the cat refuses to eat, try another brand of cat food, move its dish to another location, and be sure to rinse off all traces of soap after washing the food dish; in short, do everything you possibly can to get the cat eating again. If, in a day or two, the cat still refuses to eat, then make your phone call. Of course, there are life-threatening situations that require immediate attention. For example, if the cat is having trouble breathing, if it is bleeding, if it is vomiting repeatedly (the occasional regurgitation of a hairball is natural for a cat and should be no cause for alarm on your part), or if it has a fever or diarrhea, call the veterinarian at once.

Be observant. Get to know your cat's habits. If you are used to spending a particular part of each day with your cat but one day your cat is nowhere to be found, this itself may be a sign that something is wrong; cats sometimes have the habit of going off by themselves when they are not feeling well. If your cat or kitten continually

Get to know your cat's habits. If your normally active cat seems depressed and lethargic, for example, something may be wrong.

scratches itself, it may have fleas. If the animal constantly shakes its head, it may have ear mites. If your pet won't let you handle it, perhaps it has bruised, cut, or injured itself. Do not ignore your cat. Take notice of the same things you did when you first purchased the animal, as suggested in the section on checking for signs of good health. Is the cat eating properly? Is it having trouble keeping itself groomed? Is it using the litter pan? Does is strain to urinate or defecate? Is it having difficulty walking? Are its claws overgrown? Is it less active or vocal than usual? A daily observation of your cat or kitten is very important for the early detection of a possible problem. And keep in mind that a growing kitten or a pregnant female should be watched even more closely to make sure all is well.

The Veterinarian

As soon as you decide to bring a new cat or kitten into your home, you should select a local veterinarian who will give the cat its yearly examination and who will care for your pet should it become injured or ill. Do not wait until an emergency arises to find a good vet. There are even some veterinarians who specialize in feline medicine. Before or immediately after you purchase your cat or kitten, make an appointment with the veterinarian so that he or she can give the animal a clean bill of health. This initial examination is important for *all* cats, regardless of where they were purchased and regardless of how healthy they may appear. Most breeders of purebred, pedigreed animals will agree to let you take your new cat or kitten to a veterinarian of your own choosing within a certain time of the purchase. If the animal is found to be unhealthy in any way, it is usually agreed that it may be returned to the seller. But this agreement does not always hold true with all sellers, so it is wise to inquire about this before you pay for the animal. Even if you adopt a free kitten, you should have it examined by a veterinarian to make sure it starts out its new life with you in a healthy condition.

The most important way to protect your cat from disease is through a regular inoculation program and through periodic veterinary examinations. As already mentioned, vaccines should be given soon after a kitten is weaned from its mother, followed by booster shots throughout its life. At the time of purchase, you should question the seller as to whether your cat or kitten has been inoculated with these important vaccines. If for some reason it has not, make an appointment with the veterinarian immediately. These vaccines will stimulate the animal's own immune system so that it can build antibodies to fight off certain diseases to which it is susceptible. This precautionary measure is also important if you plan to introduce a new cat or kitten to other felines in your home.

Be certain to ask the veterinarian's advice in all matters concerning your cat or kitten's health. Do not try to medicate an animal yourself; you may cause more harm than good. Make appointments regularly for general check-ups, and consult the veterinarian in the event a problem arises.

Some Common Cat Diseases

One of the major killers among domestic cats is Feline Leukemia Virus (FeLV), for which there is no vaccine. Researchers are striving to develop one and we hope that in the not-too-distant-future our felines will be protected against this dreaded disease. FeLV tends to suppress the cat's or kitten's natural immune

In a multicat household, a sick animal (particularly one with an infectious disease) should be isolated from the rest until it is well again.

system so that the animal becomes susceptible to other diseases and disorders; this is why other diseases are often linked with FeLV. It is a highly contagious disease among cats and can be spread through contaminated saliva, urine, feces, and blood; or it can be passed from a mother cat to her kittens via her milk. Cats that live in multicat households are particularly susceptible, as are young kittens. Symptoms include anemia (evidenced by pale gums), weight loss, depression, breathing difficulty,

Keeping the Cat Healthy

swollen lymph nodes, or recurring illness, fever, or infection. This list is by no means complete; and since the symptoms vary, it is often difficult to detect FeLV in its early stages. The disease organism may be transmitted by carrier cats; that is, cats that appear healthy and do not show signs of the disease but which are capable of passing the disease to other cats. There are tests to determine the presence of FeLV in your cat or kitten; check with the veterinarian about this.

Panleukopenia (also known as feline distemper and feline infectious enteritis, among other names) is a highly contagious viral disease that is widespread. It has a high mortality rate, especially among kittens and older cats, and it is transmitted through the air and through an infected cat's urine, feces, saliva, or nasal discharges. Cats of all ages are susceptible and become infected usually through direct contact with another infected cat. Even cats that have recovered from the disease may continue to shed the virus in their feces and urine. Signs often include fever, loss of appetite, depression, vomiting, diarrhea, weight loss, and dehydration. The vomitus may appear watery and yellowish, and sometimes blood may pass with the diarrhea. The infected cat will often appear thirsty as it sits head hanging downward over its water dish, yet it will not drink. Prompt medical attention is necessary in order to save a cat's life, although even with treatment many cats die. Vaccinations are the best form of preventive medicine.

There are a number of respiratory diseases, many of which are contagious, that affect cats and kittens. Those that are especially debilitating and widespread are Feline Viral Rhinotracheitis (FVR), Calicivirus (FCV), and Pneumonitis. Symptoms are similar for all three viral diseases and may include sneezing, coughing, watery eyes, runny nose, drooling, fever, loss of appetite, depression, and mouth ulcers. The symptoms of these respiratory problems are like those of the flu or a cold in humans. Infected cats spread the virus by sneezing, thus spraying virus-laden droplets into the air. In multicat households, the virus is spread rapidly, so it is important to isolate sick individuals. The veterinarian probably will prescribe antibiotics, antihistimines (to clear the nasal passages), and perhaps nose drops and eye drops. The vaccinations for these contagious upper respiratory diseases are often given in

Keeping the Cat Healthy

conjunction with the Panleukopenia vaccination.

Although at one time Rabies was no cause for alarm among cat owners, today the disease is prevalent among the feline population, perhaps because cats typically have not been vaccinated for Rabies the way dogs have been. What is even more alarming is that Rabies is transmissible to all warm-blooded animals—including man—so it is doubly important to have your cat or kitten inoculated against this dreadful disease. It is usually transmitted through the saliva of rabid animals, and those animals that are especially likely to be carriers of Rabies are raccoons, skunks, bats, and foxes. If your cat or kitten is scratched or bitten by a rabid animal, in just a short time it may weaken and die; once the symptoms appear, there is no cure. This is one good reason why your pet should be kept indoors, particularly if you live near woods where some of these small wild creatures that might be carriers of Rabies live. Rabies may take two forms: cats that show signs of "furious" Rabies are excited, aggressive, and may suddenly attack, biting and scratching; cats that display "dumb" Rabies are usually more passive and are characterized by paralysis and a drooping jaw—the paralysis usually leads to death. Be certain to consult your veterinarian about a Rabies vaccine for your cat or kitten if your pet has not yet had one.

Other Problems

Feline Urological Syndrome (FUS), in which several symptoms may be involved, can affect cats of all ages, both male and female. One or several of the following symptoms have been known to occur: cystitis (inflammation of the bladder), urolithiasis (body fluid salts form small, sand-like particles), urethral blockage (the sand-like particles form plugs or stones, particularly in males, and prevent the passage of urine), and uremia (poisonous wastes accumulate in the blood stream as a result of the cat's inability to urinate—death can result within twenty-four hours). The exact cause of FUS is still uncertain; however, there are preventive measures which can be taken, particularly with regard to diet and exercise. These precautions can be recommended by the veterinarian. It is important to observe daily your cat's or kitten's litter pan habits. If you notice the animal straining to

Keeping the Cat Healthy

urinate or defecate (with no or few results) or failing to use the litter pan (instead, perhaps using the carpet or bathtub), or if you see bloody urine, notify the veterinarian at once.

Some cats may be plagued at one time or another with parasites, *i.e.,* fleas, ticks, mites, or worms. All warm-blooded animals can contract fleas, no matter how healthy or clean they are. If you do notice fleas on your pet, let the veterinarian know about this. He or she will probably prescribe any one of several products to eradicate the problem: flea collars, flea sprays or powders, or flea dips or shampoos. Besides de-fleaing the cat, it will be

If your cat or kitten is bothered by fleas, which appear as tiny black specks throughout the fur, it will be necessary to not only de-flea the animal, but its environment as well.

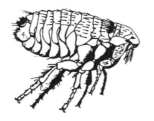

just as important to de-flea the cat's surroundings, since these pests are constantly being hatched in the environment. Be certain to seek professional advice before treating the cat.

Ticks usually are associated with outdoor cats; if you allow your cat to go outside, check its fur (especially at the roots) before you allow it to come inside.

Ticks usually are a problem with outdoor cats. These small, hard-shelled parasites attach themselves to the skin, bury their heads in it, and proceed to feed on the host's blood. If you attempt to remove a tick from your cat or kitten with forceps or tweezers, be careful to remove the entire parasite. Often the tick's body is pulled away and the head is left imbedded in the cat's skin, where it can cause an infection.

Mites can cause discomfort by irritating the ears of your cat or kitten; a periodic check of the animal's ears will determine the

Keeping the Cat Healthy

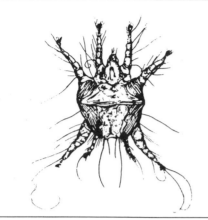

The ear mite can cause your cat or kitten great discomfort. These parasites feed on wax and debris that may have accumulated in your cat's ears, so this is why it is important to keep the animal's ears clean.

presence of ear mites (dark debris in the ear). Sometimes, however, the ear canal is clean and the mites have worked their way into the inner ear. In either case, a veterinarian should treat the animal. It is important to keep your cat's or kitten's ears clean and to consult the veterinarian immediately if you suspect a problem.

The presence of worms in an animal is usually determined by microscopic examination of the animal's stool, so when your cat has its annual check-up at the vet's, bring along a sample of your cat's stool. The vet will determine what, if any, worms are affecting your pet and will prescribe proper treatment,

if necessary. Those worms that are seen in cats are roundworms, tapeworms, hookworms, heartworms, and coccidia. Most worms will lower their hosts' resistance to disease as they rob them of important nutrients; however, with proper treatment these internal parasites can be effectively exterminated.

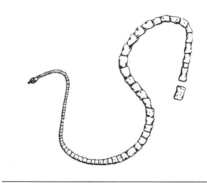

Each segment of the tapeworm is filled with eggs; as the eggs mature, the segments are passed in the cat's stool. Your veterinarian can determine the presence of tapeworms and offer an effective treatment if necessary.

First Aid and Safety

As previously mentioned, before bringing your new cat or kitten into your home, try to scan each room in search of potential dangers that might threaten your cat's life or that might injure the animal in some way. Surely you cannot think of

45

Keeping the Cat Healthy

everything, but try as much as possible to prevent accidents before they happen. Do not leave poisonous products within your cat's or kitten's reach. Place screens securely over all open windows so that if the cat or kitten decides to investigate a sunny windowsill, it won't fall out. On a hot day, never leave your pet unattended in a locked car whose windows have been tightly shut; many a cat has suffered from heat stroke as a result of its owner's negligence. Store all sewing supplies, particularly needles, far away from the animal's curious paws. These are but a few things to think about when it comes to your cat's or kitten's safety. If the animal has injured or poisoned itself, do what you can to keep it warm and comfortable until medical help can be obtained. And don't delay in contacting the veterinarian, who will want to know as much information as possible regarding the accident or problem.

Cuts and scratches usually can be administered to by the cat owner. The important thing is to clean the wound so that it does not become infected. Using a cotton swab and an antiseptic, such as hydrogen peroxide, cleanse the wound gently. Check the wound often to see that it heals properly. Unfortunately, cuts and scratches are not always easy to detect, especially if the cat is longhaired; by the time you discover the wound, it may have already become infected. Now is the time to call the vet. If the cat or kitten is bleeding profusely, as the result of a deep cut or laceration, apply a pressure bandage and rush the animal to your veterinarian who can take over and remedy the situation.

Cats are very agile creatures, but they do not always land on their feet if they fall, and not in all cases do they escape injury and broken bones. If your cat or kitten has taken a serious fall and you suspect there are broken bones, avoid moving the animal. Keep it calm and warm until the veterinarian arrives and is able to determine the severity of the problem. Do not attempt to fasten a splint to a sprained, broken, or dislocated limb; rather, allow one who is qualified in such matters—the veterinarian—to handle this procedure. There may be complications that you are unaware of, so it is best to seek professional help.

Even though a cat or kitten is safer when kept indoors, there are numerous things inside the home that can prove to be dangerous or even deadly to a curious feline. If you suspect that your cat or kitten

Keeping the Cat Healthy

has ingested poison (the animal may stagger, appear weak, vomit, or exhibit convulsions), contact the veterinarian as quickly as possible. If you know what poison was swallowed, so much the better; this information will prove helpful when you speak to the vet. Based on what you tell him, he can suggest an antidote. Cats have swallowed aspirin tablets that were left out on the counter. They have even lapped water from a toilet which has been treated with scented toilet bowl cleaners and disinfectants! Yes, cats can get into everything that they don't understand may be hazardous to their health. Try to think ahead and remove as many of those hazards as possible.

Giving the Cat a Pill

If your cat or kitten does become ill and the veterinarian prescribes medicine for you to administer to your pet, you must see to it that the cat ingests this medicine if it is to become well again. If the idea of pilling your cat seems horrifying to you, follow these instructions and ask the veterinarian for help if you still are not sure how to do it. But don't panic; many cat owners have learned how to pill a cat by

themselves with no assistance.

So the cat or kitten does not claw you while you are administering the medicine, the animal should be wrapped in a towel (a small towel will do for a kitten, a larger one for

Weight loss may indicate that there is something wrong with your cat. Do not hesitate to call your veterinarian.

47

a mature cat). Spread the towel out on a counter top and fold one of the four corners back, the way you would a baby's diaper. Place the cat on the towel, and encourage it to lie down on its stomach with its head over the edge of the fold. Now bring up the corner that is diagonally across from the fold and let it drape over the cat's back. Bring the other two corners, to the left and right of the cat, up to the middle and roll them together until the cat is securely wrapped in this "coccoon." Keep the rolled portion on top so that the cat cannot work its way out. Only the cat's head should be exposed. Hold the cat firmly in your lap in the crook of an arm so that both hands are free.

Using the thumb and forefinger of one hand, grasp the corners of the cat's mouth with slight pressure until the cat opens its mouth. With the cat's head tilted back and its mouth open, gently push the pill as far into the cat's mouth as possible with the other hand. Hold the cat's mouth shut and then gently stroke its throat. Watch to see that the cat has swallowed the pill.

Some people try placing the pill in a bit of cat food. This rarely works, as the cat usually discovers the medicine, eats the food, and leaves the pill behind in the dish.

Two of the tabby patterns seen in domestic cats are the mackerel (striped) and the classic (blotched).

Showing the Cat

If you would like to enter your cat or kitten in a cat show sponsored by one of the various cat registering associations listed at the end of this chapter, you are in luck. Shows are held almost every weekend throughout the year in every part of the country. And, as previously mentioned, you need not enter a purebred, pedigreed show cat; there are also household pet shows for mixed breeds and these are often held in conjunction with the championship shows for purebred cats. But whether the cat or kitten entered is purebred or not, it must be the picture of good health and in good show condition. Proper diet, exercise, regular grooming sessions, and strict attention to the cat's or kitten's health and welfare figure importantly in keeping the animal in top condition. At vetted shows, each entry must be examined at the show entrance by a veterinarian before it is admitted to the show hall. Cats that have been declawed or that appear unhealthy—especially those that show signs of infectious disease—are automatically disqualified. These veterinary inspections are an important precautionary measure to ensure that disease does not spread among the great numbers of show entries that are admitted. You can do your

The Oriental Shorthair, in this case a spotted tabby, is long and slender with a short fine-textured coat.

part by having your cat or kitten vaccinated against the major cat diseases before it starts its show career.

The reasons for entering a cat or kitten in a show may vary from person to person, but remember to keep the animal's best interests in mind at all times. Cat shows are where some of the finest specimens can be seen side by side, where exhibitors can see just how well their cats and kittens measure up to others of their kind. In the case of purebred, pedigreed show animals, every entry is judged according to a

Showing the Cat

written standard of perfection. Each cat registering association develops its own set of standards, one for each of the breeds it recognizes for championship. Each breed standard describes what a perfect specimen of that breed should look like; and every breeder of purebred cats and kittens strives to produce in their animals those ideal qualities that are called for in the standard of their particular breed. Of course there are no perfect specimens, but many come close to perfection. Show judges use these standards as a guide to help them make their decisions; breeders use the standards to help them develop various breeding strategies that will improve their stock; and exhibitors study the standards to see how well their animals measure up to the ideal. Cats and kittens that are shown as household pets are judged solely on their beauty and condition, not against a written standard, and household pet entries are judged separately from purebred, pedigreed entries.

Cat shows are by no means small events when one considers the tremendous amount of work that is involved. Often these shows are planned several months to a year in advance. Cat clubs that are affiliated with one of the several cat

A black and white bi-color Scottish Fold with the characteristic folded ears that sit atop a rounded head.

registering associations and that wish to sponsor a show must first gain approval from the registering body's central office before the rest of the show details can be worked out. Among other things, a suitable show hall must be located and reserved, judges must be selected, arrangements must be made with the various vendors who will set up booths at the show, entry forms must be sent out and then compiled as they are returned, trophies and awards must be ordered, show catalogs must be planned and printed, show cages and other cage accessories that will be furnished for entries must be secured, and, of course, the show must be

Showing the Cat

publicized. And the list of preparations could go on.

If you want to show your cat, find out what shows have been planned for the year, what the show dates are, and who to contact for information. Local cat clubs and cat magazines are good sources for information regarding cat shows. Perhaps a veterinarian or local animal shelter could help you get in touch with a cat fancier who could share some details about upcoming shows. Or you might want to ask the seller of your cat or kitten for show information. Once you have decided on the show that you would like to enter, write to the show club's entry clerk and request an entry form. Take care to fill out the form accurately, as this information will appear in the show catalog and the judges' books. The completed form, along with the appropriate fees, should be mailed back to the entry clerk as soon as possible. Make certain that you receive a copy of the show rules and regulations (these should be read over very carefully) to find out what is required of you as an exhibitor, how the judging procedure works, when the judging will take place, and so on. You should receive a confirmation that your entry fee and form were received by the entry clerk and that you have been accepted as an exhibitor. Now sit back and wait for the big day!

Once you plan to show your cat, you will have to make that extra effort to keep your cat or kitten in prime condition so that it is presented at its best before the judges on show day. All entries should be groomed to perfection; many are often bathed before each show. The coat of a show cat must be spotlessly clean, shiny, and free of tangles, mats, external parasites (such as fleas), and dirt. Longhaired cats and kittens will need far more grooming attention than their shorthaired counterparts, simply because their coats are more difficult

This domestic shorthaired cat exhibits a mackerel tabby coat pattern. The tabby markings extend onto the facial area as well.

to care for and to keep clean. Many exhibitors prefer to bathe their cats or kittens several days or so before the main event; in this way, some of the natural oils that help keep a coat shiny are restored. Others give their show cats or kittens a dry bath with powder to absorb the excess oil in the fur. It is this excess oil that tends to attract dirt and dust, which in turn gives the animal an untidy appearance. If powder is used, be sure to brush it through the fur so that there are no traces left for the judges to see. The amount of grooming necessary to make your cat or kitten look its best will depend on the length, texture, and color of its coat and how skilled the animal is in keeping its own coat clean. And remember to remove any wax that may have accumulated in your cat's or kitten's ears, to wipe away matter that may have collected in the corners of the eyes, and to remove any stains that may have occurred beneath the chin (from eating) or on the foot pads. Claws should be clipped short before the show, and the animal should receive a final brushing and combing to remove loose, dead hair. As mentioned previously, grooming should be part of the normal routine of caring for your cat; do not wait until a show rolls around to start

getting the cat's coat in good order. And remember, show cats at an early age should become accustomed to handling (since they will be handled by strangers at the show), to being confined in a cage, and to traveling.

As the show day approaches, assemble the grooming tools, a sturdy cat carrier, cat food, a bottle of water, food and water dishes, some of the cat's or kitten's favorite toys, and some food and drink for yourself, together with whatever else you think will be needed to make both you and your feline comfortable. Some shows provide cat food and dishes and litter pans and litter, along with the regulation show cages; however, some may not. Check out these details beforehand in the show rules and regulations. Even if a show provides food and water, it might be a good idea to bring your own just in case your cat or kitten decides to be finicky about what it eats and drinks that day. You will probably be required to bring along some sort of a cover for the show cage, whose dimensions should be included somewhere in the show rules and regulations. The cover can be as simple as a large bath towel, or it can be as elaborate as custom-made curtains. Be sure to bring along some clips or

Showing the Cat

clothespins with which to fasten the cover to the cage. You may also want to bring along a small rug or towel to line the bottom of the show cage, so that your cat or kitten will be more comfortable.

At the time you fill out the show entry form, you will probably be asked to check the particular class in which you plan to enter your cat or kitten. If you are uncertain about this, ask the entry clerk. As already mentioned, household pets are usually judged separately from purebred, pedigreed animals. With purebred, pedigreed animals, the story is different. Kittens are usually judged separately from adult cats. Cats that have been neutered and spayed are judged in still a separate class, and there are individual classes for cats that have earned points toward their championship and those individuals that have earned points toward grand championship.

Your cat or kitten will probably be entered in one of two shows—a specialty show, in which perhaps only one breed competes or in which either shorthaired or longhaired cats compete, or an all-breed show, in which several breeds are judged against each other. Your entry will be judged first against others of its kind; that is, others in its class and breed. Males and females are usually judged separately. Several judges may take a turn to evaluate your entry, and then each judge will select his or her class winners, usually by placing ribbons on the cages of those winning entries. Winners in each class within a particular breed compete for a best of breed award, and then the judging narrows down as the best of breed winners compete until one cat is finally judged the best cat in show. Judging procedures vary from association to association, but generally the process is similar.

In most cat shows, it is important to remain silent when your cat or kitten is called to the ring to be judged. Listen carefully as the judge talks about the good and bad qualities of your entry. Much can be learned at this point if you keep an open mind. Later, after the judging is over, you may wish to ask questions. Most judges will be more than happy to discuss your entry with you briefly, although they are under no obligation to do so. Even if you and your cat or kitten don't come home with ribbons and trophies, at least the animal will have gained a point score based on its breed standard (if it is a purebred, pedigreed cat or kitten).

53

Showing the Cat

These points can work toward the cat's or kitten's championship and grand championship if this is the goal you have in mind for your show cat.

Whether you win or lose is not important; the feeling of pride you'll get just from exhibiting your cat or kitten should be what counts!

The following is a list of the major cat registering associations that sanction cat shows all across the country. In most instances, every cat or kitten entered in a show must be registered with the particular association that is sponsoring the show. We have eliminated the addresses since these are apt to change frequently. You might find their addresses in *Cats* or *Cat Fancy* magazines, or perhaps a veterinarian, local animal shelter, or the person from whom you purchased your cat or kitten could give you this information.

American Cat Association (ACA)
American Cat Fanciers' Association (ACFA)
Canadian Cat Association
Cat Fanciers' Association (CFA)
Cat Fanciers' Federation (CFF)
Crown Cat Fanciers' Federation (CROWN)

The International Cat Association (TICA)
United Cat Federation (UCF)

The Cat Fanciers' Association, Inc. (CFA) is the largest and one of the oldest cat registering associations in the United States. Following are samples of two breed standards that were adopted by CFA, which appear in their *Show Standards* booklet. Other cat registering organizations publish breed standards which in some ways are similar to the ones included here.

Abyssinian cats are known for their beautiful ticked coats, whereby each individual hair is banded with alternating colors. Any evidence of dark tabby markings on a show specimen is considered a fault by some cat registering associations.

Showing the Cat

ABYSSINIAN

POINT SCORE

HEAD (25)
Muzzle 6
Skull 6
Ears 7
Eye Shape 6

BODY (30)
Torso 15
Legs and Feet 10
Tail 5

COAT (10)
Texture 10

COLOR (35)
Color 15
Ticking 15
Eye Color 5

GENERAL: The overall impression of the ideal Abyssinian would be a colorful cat with a distinctly ticked coat, medium in size and regal in appearance. The Abyssinian is lithe, hard and muscular, showing eager activity and a lively interest in all surroundings. Well-balanced temperamentally and physically with all elements of the cat in proportion.

HEAD: A modified, slightly rounded wedge without flat planes; the brow, cheek, and profile lines all showing a gentle contour. A slight rise from the bridge of the nose to the forehead, which should be of good size, with width between the ears and flowing into the arched neck without a break.

MUZZLE: Not sharply pointed or square. The chin should be neither receding nor protruding. Allowance should be made for jowls in adult males.

EARS: Alert, large, and moderately pointed; broad, and cupped at base and set as though listening. Hair on ears very short and close-lying, preferably tipped with black or dark brown on a ruddy Aybssinian or chocolate-brown on a red Abyssinian.

EYES: Almond-shaped, large, brilliant, and expressive. Neither round nor Oriental. Eyes accentuated by dark lidskin, encircled by light-colored area.

BODY: Medium long, lithe and graceful, but showing well-developed muscular strength without coarseness. Abyssinian conformation strikes a medium between the extremes of the cobby and the svelte lengthy type. Proportion and general balance more to be desired than mere size.

LEGS AND FEET: Proportionately slim, fine boned. The Abyssinian stands well off the ground giving the impression of being on tip toe. Paws small, oval, and compact. Toes, five in front and four behind.

TAIL: Thick at base, fairly long and tapering.

COAT: Soft, silky, fine in texture, but dense and resilient to the touch with a lustrous sheen. Medium in length but long enough to accommodate two or three bands of ticking.

PENALIZE: Off-color pads. Long narrow head. Short round head. Barring on legs. Rings on tail. Coldness or grey tones in coat.

DISQUALIFY: White locket, or white anywhere other than nostril, chin, and upper throat area. Kinked or abnormal tail. Dark unbroken necklace. Grey undercoat close to the skin extending throughout a major portion of the body. Any black hair on red Abyssinian. Incorrect number of toes.

ABYSSINIAN COLORS

RUDDY: Coat ruddy brown, ticked with various shades of darker brown or black; the extreme outer tip to be the darkest, with orange-brown undercoat, ruddy to the skin. Darker shading along spine allowed if fully ticked. Tail tipped with black and without rings. The undersides and forelegs (inside) to be a tint to harmonize with the main color. Preference given to *unmarked* orange-brown (burnt-sienna) color. Nose Leather: Tile Red. Paw Pads: Black or brown, with black between toes and extending slightly beyond the paws. Eye Color: Gold or green, the more richness and depth of color the better.

RED: Warm, glowing red, distinctly ticked with chocolate-brown. Deeper shades of red preferred. However, good ticking not to be sacrificed merely for depth of color. Ears and tail tipped with chocolate-brown. Nose Leather: Rosy pink. Paw Pads: Pink, with chocolate-brown between toes, extending slightly beyond paws. Eye Color: Gold or green, the more richness and depth of color the better.

Allowable outcross breeds - None.

Showing the Cat

BURMESE

GENERAL: The overall impression of the ideal Burmese would be a cat of medium size and rich, solid sable color with substantial bone structure, good muscular development and a surprising weight for its size. This together with expressive eyes and a sweet expression presents a totally distinctive cat which is comparable to no other breed. Perfect physical condition, with excellent muscle tone. There should be no evidence of obesity, paunchiness, weakness, or apathy.

HEAD, EARS, and EYES: Head pleasingly rounded without flat planes whether viewed from the front or side. The face is full with considerable breadth between the eyes and blends gently into a broad, well-developed short muzzle that maintains the rounded contours of the head. In profile there is a visible nose break. The chin is firmly rounded, reflecting a proper bite. The head sits on a well-developed neck. The ears are medium in size, set well apart, broad at the base and rounded at the tips. Tilting slightly forward, the ears contribute to an alert appearance. The eyes are large, set far apart, with rounded aperture.

BODY: Medium in size, muscular in development, and presenting a compact appearance. Allowance to be made for larger size in males. An ample, rounded chest, with back level from shoulder to tail.

LEGS: Well proportioned to body.

PAWS: Round. Toes, five in front and four behind.

TAIL: Straight, medium in length.

COAT: Fine, glossy, satin-like texture, short and very close lying.

COLOR: The mature specimen is a rich, warm, sable brown, shading almost imperceptibly to a slightly lighter hue on the underparts but otherwise without shadings, barring, or markings of any kind. (Kittens are often lighter in color.) Nose leather and paw pads are brown. Eye color ranges from gold to yellow, the greater the depth and brilliance the better. Green eyes are a fault.

DISQUALIFY: Kinked or abnormal tail, lockets or spots. Blue eyes. Incorrect number of toes. Incorrect nose leather or paw pad color. Malocclusion of the jaw that results in a severe underbite or overbite that visually prohibits the described profile and/or, malformation that results in protruding teeth or a wry face or jaw.

Color Captions

This healthy specimen is bright-eyed and alert; its coat is clean and shiny, page 57. Cats and kittens love the outdoors, but be careful not to allow your pet to roam beyond the boundaries of your property, page 58. "Patches," a household pet, and her kitten, page 59. A Burmese queen nurses her litter of six, pages 60 and 61. Seal point Himalayan. Color points are restricted to the face, the ears, the lower legs, the paws, and the tail, page 62. A trio of longhaired kittens, page 63. Cats that live in the country or on farms are great mousers. This hard worker enjoys a respite from a long day's work, page 64.

Breeding the Cat

If your goal is to breed your male or female cat or perhaps to start a cattery of your own, then you should search for the finest quality animals that you can, animals that are healthy and in excellent condition and that carry good qualities in their bloodlines. If you plan to breed purebred, show-quality cats, then you should brush up on your genetics, study the various pedigrees of the top show cats, go to cat shows where you can see these fine specimens, talk to other breeders, and seek the advice of a veterinarian before you begin. Also keep in mind that some breeder-quality cats are not capable of winning in the show ring, but they *are* capable of producing offspring that will win shows. Breeding, whether on a large or small scale, is not for beginners. With purebred, pedigreed cats especially, it takes years to develop a particular line, and to produce high-quality show cats demands a lot of time and money. Compared to the expenses that are encountered, profits from selling these cats are usually low; you will be lucky just to break even. One does not venture into the world of breeding purebred cats with the idea of making money but instead with a love for cats and with a desire to see a particular breed strengthened (improved) according to the breed's standard of perfection.

There are several strategies from which to choose when you breed cats. Inbreeding cats (mating father to daughter or mother to son, for example) is usually done in order to maintain certain desirable features; however, too much close inbreeding sometimes reduces the vigor and stamina of successive generations of cats. Through careful inbreeding programs, you can "lock in" those desirable qualities and predict with certainty what the offspring will look like and, to an extent, what the temperaments will be like; nonetheless, there is always the chance that undesirable qualities will also show up. There is always this risk. Outcrossing, mating cats from two different lines, or strains, is normally done when a breeder wants to try to bring in a specific trait or feature. There is more of a gamble involved with outcrossing, since you are combining different bloodlines; but by closely inspecting the cats potentially to be outcrossed and by thoroughly examining their pedigrees, successful results can be achieved. Line-breeding, mating cats of the same bloodline but that are not closely related (niece to uncle, grandson to grandmother and so

Breeding the Cat

on), is used to maintain and gradually improve a strain. It is probably the most frequently used breeding method, and it is especially good for novices who do not have a lot of experience with the breed and its various bloodlines.

The Estrous Cycle

Sexually mature female cats have periodic cycles every few weeks, and during these cycles the hormone estrogen is responsible for producing signs of "heat." Often a female cat in heat will roll around on the ground, tread the ground with her paws, cry loudly, and generally be restless and difficult to handle. She will demand to be let outdoors to greet her male suitors who will gladly come from miles to mate with her. She may even spray urine on various objects, much to the dismay of her owner. If you want to breed your female cat, check with the veterinarian first. He or she will be able to determine if the cat is mature enough to be bred. If your female is in breeding condition, do not let her wander outside where many dangers await her and where any tomcat is capable of siring her kittens. Keep her indoors where it is safe and warm, and arrange to have her mated with a male cat of your own choosing. Owners of purebred, pedigreed females often seek the services of an available stud cat (a sexually mature male cat that is used in breeding programs) to mate with their queens. There is usually a stud fee and arrangements have to be made in advance. If mating occurs and it is successful, ovulation will follow in a female cat that is fertile, and the estrous cycle will terminate until after the kittens are born.

Mating

Before you allow your cat to mate with a member of the opposite sex, both animals will need some time to get to know each other. When it is certain that a queen is in heat, allow both the male and female to come in close contact with one another in a quiet room, away from outside disturbances. Many breeders will often place each animal in a separate enclosure in the same room so that they can see, hear, and smell each other. When the animals seem receptive to one another, they are let out of the enclosures to further investigate their surroundings and each other. Female cats in heat will give off a scent that is particularly

Breeding the Cat

attractive to the sexually mature male. The male will make advances, but he may be rejected a few times until the female feels she is ready. To indicate her readiness to mate, the queen will roll around on the floor and lie down on her stomach, treading the floor with her paws and thrusting her hindquarters up in the usual mating stance. The male will then mount the female, biting her on the scruff of the neck and grasping her sides with his paws. He will insert his penis into her vagina with several hard thrusts. The penis is covered with small barb-like projections and these may be painful for the female during copulation, as evidenced by her loud cries. After the animals have copulated, the male withdraws, dismounts, and if he is experienced at mating quickly jumps aside to avoid a sudden swipe of the female's claws. Both animals quickly lick and clean their genital areas. As they begin to lose interest in each other, they are separated. Breeders of purebred cats will often allow the queen and stud to mate several times just to be certain the female was indeed impregnated.

Gestation

It is important for a pregnant queen to avoid other sexually mature males after she has been mated with the male of your choosing, since she is still capable of mating and of being fertilized again. If this were to happen, her litter of kittens could conceivably be sired by more than one male. Gestation, the period in which the kittens develop in their mother's womb, may last from eight to ten weeks, depending on the individual cat or the particular breed of cat. The queen will be begin to grow larger and rounder, gaining weight as the kittens grow and her appetite increases. Let her eat all she wants, so that the kittens growing inside her will receive proper nourishment. Each kitten will develop in its own amniotic sac filled with fluid; and each one will receive its oxygen, blood supply, and nourishment through its individual umbilical cord and the placenta, which connects the fetus to the lining of the queen's uterus. The queen's nipples will become more prominent in size and they will appear dark pink in color as the mammary glands swell with milk.

The queen will become less active as the gestation period continues.

Breeding the Cat

She will search for a place to give birth to her litter. This is the time to provide her with her own "nest" before she decides to give birth in your linen closet or on a pile of clean laundry in the basement or in the middle of your bed! Offer her a place that is acceptable to you. A large, sturdy, clean box will do, one in which the queen can stretch out and feel comfortable. Place the box in a dimly lit, dry, warm, secure place, free from drafts and away from household activities. Keep a close watch on the queen and make certain not to leave her alone and not to let her outside.

Parturition

Do not disturb a queen giving birth to her kittens, but make yourself available to her in case she may need your assistance. Make sure the veterinarian is available too, in case there are complications during delivery of the kittens. You will know when the birth of the kittens is imminent because the queen will remain in her box for long intervals of time. She may refuse to eat. Contractions will begin, and the animal will begin to pant and cry. After several contractions, a kitten will emerge enveloped in a fluid-filled membrane, the amniotic sac. This membrane usually ruptures upon delivery; if it does not, the queen will tear it open. It is important that the kitten start breathing immediately—it cannot do so if it is still surrounded by a membrane full of fluid. If for some reason the queen fails to tear open the membrane, you may have to help. The queen will begin to vigorously lick the remnants of fluid off the newborn kitten to stimulate its breathing and blood circulation. She will continue to lick the kitten until it is clean. The kittens should be followed by the placenta. The queen will eat this source of protein; do not be alarmed if you see her do this, as it is perfectly normal behavior. Make certain that the placenta follows the birth of the kittens; if this is not the case, notify the veterinarian at once. Normally the queen will sever the umbilical cord. If she fails to do this, you may have to step in with a pair of sterilized scissors and cut the umbilical cord yourself. It is better to have a veterinarian on hand for this procedure, if possible.

As each kitten is cleaned off by the queen and starts breathing on its own, it instinctively finds its way to a nipple and starts to nurse. It is

Breeding the Cat

important for the newborn kittens to receive this first milk (colostrum). Watch each kitten to see that it finds a nipple to suck. Before the kittens are due, you might want to trim some of the fur that surrounds the queen's nipples so that the kittens will not have difficulty finding their food source. Avoid handling or moving the kittens. Allow them to stay with their mother in the nest. Offer assistance only if you suspect there is a problem, and call a veterinarian if you are in doubt about anything. If the queen has contractions for several hours without producing any results, if the kittens are having difficulty exiting the birth canal, if a kitten is stillborn, or if the kit fails to nurse, do not hesitate to call the veterinarian. Do not try to handle these complications of labor and delivery by yourself.

The New Family

Provide the queen with fresh food and water each day and be sure to keep her litter pan nearby so that she does not have to wander away from her youngsters. The mother will take care of her kittens' toilet habits first by licking their genital areas to stimulate urination and defecation. Then she will consume their wastes after each meal. Be sure to continue feeding the queen an enriched diet high in protein and calcium. Check with the veterinarian about the queen's diet. It is important for her to receive the proper nutrients so that she can pass them along to her nursing kittens. Try not to disturb the new family during these first few days together.

In a week or so the kittens' eyes will open and they will be able to hear noises. You will be surprised at how quickly these furry little creatures develop. You may want to weigh the kittens at regular intervals to ensure that they are steadily gaining weight. It makes sense to keep records on the kittens' progress from day to day. In a few weeks, if all goes well, the kittens will be up and around, exploring their new surroundings. Their baby teeth will come through and they will be able to start eating solid food, until gradually they are weaned from their mother's milk. But let the queen decide when the kittens should be weaned. If the mother herself is litter pan trained, she will show her kittens what is expected of them. Soon they will catch on. She will teach them how to clean themselves by licking the fur. This is why it is so crucial to leave the

Breeding the Cat

kittens with their mother until they mature enough to take care of themselves. Check with the veterinarian about the kittens' specific dietary needs as they grow, and make an appointment with him to set up an inoculation schedule for the youngsters. Soon the kittens will seem more interested in their environment than their mother and littermates. When they are self-feeding, they can safely be removed from their family, at approximately eight to ten weeks of age, and placed in new homes. Or you may fall in love with these little devils and decide to keep them yourself. If you do decide to sell them or give them away, be sure they go to loving homes where they will be taken care of in the same way you cared for them.

Altering the Cat

If you do not want to breed your cat, then the animal should be altered by a veterinarian. Many people feel that it is only necessary to spay a female cat, since it is she that will bear the kittens; this, however, is a rather narrow view of reality. Sexually mature male cats, if they are allowed outdoors to roam the neighborhood, can impregnate every available unaltered female cat for miles around. Why allow a male cat to do this? Why allow lots of unwanted kittens, kittens for whom homes might not be found, to enter this world? If you seek in your cat or kitten those qualities of household pet and family companion, and if you really love the animal, then by all means have it altered. You will be doing both yourself and the cat a favor, and at the same time you will be doing the community in which you live a great service also. Altered cats tend to be more calm and affectionate; they are less inclined to wander off in search of members of the opposite sex; and they are less likely to spray urine. Altered cats make wonderful pets.

Cat Breeds

There are dozens of breeds of purebred cats that can be seen today, most of which are the product of careful selective breeding. Not all of these pure breeds are recognized for championship by all cat registering associations, but those that *are* recognized and shown are judged according to how well they conform to their individual breed standard of perfection. There are the natural breeds, such as Abyssinians, Siamese, Maine Coons, and Russian Blues, that evolved long ago without man's intervention. Then there are the established breeds, like the Burmese and the Havana Brown, which man had a hand in creating. Hybrids, which are the product of crossing two or more breeds, and mutations, which are accidents by nature, are also seen. The

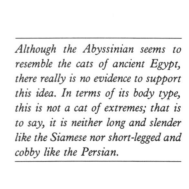

Although the Abyssinian seems to resemble the cats of ancient Egypt, there really is no evidence to support this idea. In terms of its body type, this is not a cat of extremes; that is to say, it is neither long and slender like the Siamese nor short-legged and cobby like the Persian.

Cat Breeds

Himalayan, the result of a Siamese-Persian cross, belongs to the group of hybrid breeds, while the Manx, the Scottish Fold, and the Rex breeds are considered to be mutations. Following are sections on some of the breeds of purebred cats.

Abyssinian

The Abyssinian body type strikes a happy medium, as it is neither long and slender like the Siamese, nor cobby like the longhaired Persian. The Aby is a medium-sized cat, muscular, active, and interested in its surroundings. Probably its most outstanding feature is its ticked coat, in which each individual hair is banded with alternating colors. If you were to run your hands over an Abyssinian's dense, resilient coat, you would see in the ruddy varieties bands of black (or dark brown) and orange-brown; in the red varieties you would see bands of chocolate brown and copper. (There are also other color varieties that have developed in Abyssinians.) The ticking gives the fur an iridescent quality that is quite beautiful. Eye color is typically a rich gold or green. The Abyssinian has a wild look which is appealing to many people, and some say it resembles a miniature cougar.

There is no proof that Abyssinians were first seen thousands of years ago in ancient Egypt or nearby Abyssinia (now Ethiopia), but it is easy to believe that they did come from this part of the world since they resemble some of the cats that were portrayed in the art of these early cultures.

Burmese

The rich sable-brown coat and glowing golden eyes are what one first notices about this unique breed. It is believed that Burmese cats as we know them today were developed in the United States, the first cats being descendants of Wong Mau, a brown cat (Siamese hybrid) imported from Burma. Although Burmese have been bred in other colors, it was sable that was first seen in these cats and it remains the most popular color in the U.S. today. Here these beautiful brown felines are bred as medium-sized, compact, solidly-build specimens; whereas in Britain, Burmese that are more streamlined, like the Siamese, are preferred. The Burmese should not be confused with the Havana Brown, which is bred with green eyes (rather than yellow or gold), and whose coat lacks the sheen for which Burmese are known. Also, Havanas tend to be a reddish mahoghany brown, as opposed to the deep dark sable brown seen in the Burmese breed. And Burmese have nothing to do with the Birman (the Sacred Cat of Burma); the latter is a longhaired breed with Siamese-like markings.

Himalayan

Several decades ago someone decided to cross a Siamese with a

The Cat Fanciers' Association (CFA) show standard for the Burmese breed calls for a medium-sized cat with golden eyes and a dark brown glossy coat that feels like satin. Other cat registering associations, however, may accept for championship other colors besides sable brown.

Persian to achieve a cat with characteristics of both breeds. The result? A longhaired feline with

Cat Breeds

Persian type and Siamese markings. So it was, and this hybrid breed came to be known as the Himalayan. Some cat registering associations here and abroad do not recognize the Himalayan as a separate breed, but merely as another color within the Persian class. In fact, the British refer to these cats as Colorpoint Longhairs (Longhairs are Persians in Britain). But even though Himalayans are considered a separate breed in some registering organizations, their breed standard is quite similar to that of the Persian. The broad, round head; the large, round eyes; the short, snub nose with a nose break; the small ears set far apart and low on the head; the short, cobby body supported by stocky legs; the long, flowing coat are traits that can be seen in both breeds. These magnificent blue-eyed creatures are distinguished by their color points (the facial mask, the ears, legs, feet, and tail) and they can be seen in most of the Siamese colors and

Some cat fanciers feel that with the Himalayan breed, they have the best of both worlds: the dramatic color points of the Siamese, and the body type and coat length of the Persian.

more. Himalayans should not be confused with the Balinese, a longhaired Siamese cat that evolved as a mutation. Balinese have in common with Himalayans only the colored points and silky hair texture.

Maine Coon

Many legends surround this rugged breed, which originated in the northeastern section of the United States a century ago. They are stocky cats—although they are not as colossal as some people make them out to be—and they are characterized by shaggy, heavy coats, which can be seen in a variety of colors and patterns. Perhaps it is the brown tabby's bushy tail marked with dark rings or the ability of some individuals to sit up on their haunches that led to the myth about a domestic cat mating with a raccoon, thereby creating the "coon" cat. A more probable explanation, and one accepted by many people today, is that Maine Coons evolved from matings of shorthaired and longhaired cats. Nature equipped these hardy Maine Coons with a protective coat so that they could endure the harsh New England winters.

These cats do not require the daily grooming attention that is demanded of other longhaired breeds such as the Persian and the Himalayan. Only parts of their sturdy bodies (the neck ruff, the stomach, the britches) are covered with long fur; the fur is shorter on the face and legs, and over the shoulders. Many members of the breed exhibit unusually long ear tufts, whiskers, and eyebrows.

Manx

Lots of folklore surrounds this tailless breed of cat, which, in all likelihood, developed as a mutation on the Isle of Man. Matings of tailless cats that landed on the island's shores and native shorthaired cats led to the breed's birth. Whether these cats sailed with Noah on the ark or took part in the Spanish Armada are stories based on conjecture. What *is* certain and unmistakable about these sturdy cats is their physical conformation to their breed standard, *i.e.,* their broad chests, deep flanks, short backs, and rounded rumps supported by long hind legs. The powerful hind legs and raised rump may explain why the Manx appears to hop when it runs.

Not all Manx are tailless; some individuals sport a mere stump of a

Cat Breeds

tail, while others have noticeably short tails or normal long tails. Manx breeders are careful when developing their breeding strategies, since taillessness is associated with a lethal gene. This is why breeders will often mate tailless Manx to tailed Manx in order to prevent deformities in kittens while at the same time preserving the breed's vitality. Manx are very muscular

Notice the long hind legs, the raised rump, the absence of a tail, the short compact body, and the deep chest—all characteristics that are unique to the Manx breed.

cats, covered with handsome thick, double coats. Most often the shorthaired varieties are seen, although there are also longhaired Manx, known as Cymrics, available today.

Cat Breeds

Persian

Not all longhaired cats are Persians; there is a particular head and body type that sets this popular breed apart from other longhaired varieties. The word *round* is used to describe the Persian, particularly the head: its head is round and massive; the eyes are large and round; the ears are small, rounded, and fit neatly into the contour of the head. The broad nose is short and snub with a "break" (an indentation). The thick coat of long, fine-textured hair covers a short, cobby, rounded body set on short, thick legs. The full tail rounds out the picture of what many people consider to be a very glamorous cat. When the longhaired coat is kept well groomed by the Persian owner, this breed is indeed truly beautiful.

The Persian should not be

Perisan cats are known for their luxurious flowing coats, but these handsome cats are not suitable for everyone—their long hair must be carefully brushed and combed each day in order to keep the cat looking its best.

Cat Breeds

confused with the Turkish Angora, another longhaired breed, although these two breeds may have developed simultaneously in the same part of the world centuries ago. Some experts believe that the Persian owes the silkiness of its coat to the Angora, with which it may have been bred at one time. Underneath this long, flowing coat is a solid, muscular cat with a regal appearance. Persians can be bred in a great many colors and patterns.

Rex

Those delicate, fine-boned, curly cats with the large ears and crinkled whiskers resemble the ancient Egyptian goddess Bastet, according to some experts. Most Rex cats seen in the United States today belong to one of two Rex strains: Devon or Cornish. The rex mutation first appeared in Cornwall, England (Cornish Rex), and a few years later a second rex strain emerged (Devon Rex) with a slightly different coat texture and density. In either case, Rex cats are characterized by a close-lying marcel-wave coat, which many breeders say has to be felt to be believed. The hairs are extremely soft and silky to the touch, perhaps because these cats lack the stiff

outer guard hairs that are found in most other cat breeds. In type, these small-to-medium-sized cats are similar to the Siamese. The head is longer than it is wide; and the torso, legs, and tail are long and slender. Because the short, fine-textured coat does not offer protection against the elements the way the coat of a normal (non-rex) shorthaired cat does, the Rex should be kept indoors where it is warm, especially during inclement weather. Rex are bred in a wide variety of colors and patterns.

Russian Blue

The plushy double coat makes the Russian Blue appear heavier than it really is. They are fine-boned, slender cats, however, and characterized as having foreign type (like the Siamese). There are other blue cats, like the Chartreux and the Korat, but what distinguishes the Russian Blue from these other breeds is its luxurious, thick, silver-blue coat. The Chartreux is a stockier cat, and the Korat has a sleek, fine-textured coat, although it has the luminous green eyes and the silver-tipped short hair of the Russian Blue. It is believed that the Russian Blue breed originated in the

78

Cat Breeds

Archangel section of Russia, but no one is certain. Its thick, protective coat and blue skin certainly are hints that this breed may have come from a northern climate. Bred in one color, Blues tend to be very quiet and shy; this is why they should be handled often while they are young.

Siamese

While a number of cat breeds are unfamiliar to many people, surely the Siamese, with its sapphire blue eyes, elegant svelte body, and dramatic coloring, comes to mind as one of the most popular breeds in the United States today.

This talkative, extroverted breed at one time could be seen with kinked tails and crossed eyes, but through selective breeding efforts, these traits have been bred out for the most part. Long-legged and lean, Siamese are medium-sized cats whose dark points (face mask, ears, lower legs, feet, and tail) contrast with a lighter body color. Originally bred as seal points, modern-day Siamese also can be seen wearing points of other colors such as chocolate, blue, lilac, lynx, and tortie. What is important in a purebred breeding program is to

The Siamese head is a long tapering wedge.

achieve on one animal all points of the same color limited to well-defined areas on the body.

As with many breeds, Siamese origins are shrouded in mystery; however, there is no doubt that these cats flourished for a time in Siam (now Thailand) and that some of the first Siamese imported from there went to England. Whether these cats were sacred to the people of Siam or whether they established residency in the royal palaces is uncertain.

Cat Breeds

Scottish Fold

Most members of this breed seen today can trace their ancestry to Susie, a white female with folded ears that appeared one day on a Scottish farm. Since the fold-ear gene is a mutation and since it may be responsible for producing deformities, particularly when folds are mated to folds, breeders have resorted to crossing their Scottish Folds with normal (straight-eared) domestic shorthaired cats (such as American Shorthairs and British Shorthairs) to get their desired results. Folds have a wide-eyed, sweet look that radiates from a rounded head capped with the characteristic ears that bend forward and down. The fold-ear gene is dominant, so if one parent carrys the trait, a percentage of the kittens in a litter are sure to have folded ears. The degree to which the ears actually fold is something else: some Scottish Folds exhibit tightly folded ears, so tight that the ears appear flat against the cat's head; some individuals have rather loosely flapped ears; others are straight-eared Folds, in the same way some Manx have tails.

Turkish Angora

Persians and Turkish Angoras have often been mistaken for one another, especially by people who are not familiar with the cat fancy. Actually, these two separate breeds developed centuries ago; the origin of the former is unclear, but the latter developed in the Turkish city of Ankara. At one point in history, Turkish Angoras may have been used in Persian breeding programs to establish the long, *silky* hair trait for which Angoras are known. Some authorities maintain that Turkish Angoras made their way to America and were instrumental in the development of the Maine Coon cat.

Through interbreeding with other cats, the Turkish Angora as a breed all but disappeared for a number of years, and the word *angora* was used loosely to describe various longhaired cats. But Turkish Angoras made their way back into the cat fancy scene and many fine representatives of the breed can be seen today. These medium-sized cats have long bodies and large tufted ears that sit high on wide wedge-shaped heads. The silky smooth coat together with the regal neck ruff are what makes the Turkish Angora so distinctive among felines.